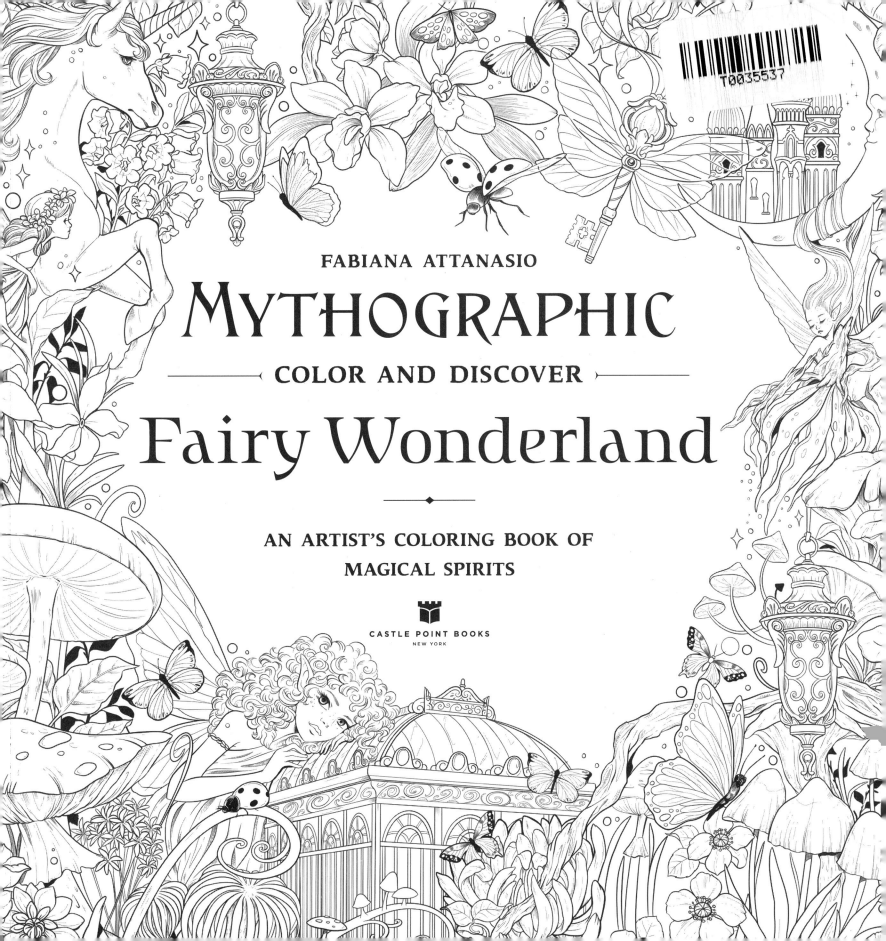

FABIANA ATTANASIO

MYTHOGRAPHIC

COLOR AND DISCOVER

Fairy Wonderland

AN ARTIST'S COLORING BOOK OF
MAGICAL SPIRITS

CASTLE POINT BOOKS
NEW YORK

Discover more of Mythographic

ISBN 978-1-250-28912-4 (trade paperback)

Cover design by Young Lim
Edited by Monica Sweeney

Our books may be purchased in bulk for promotional, educational, or business use.
Please contact your local bookseller or the Macmillan Corporate
and Premium Sales Department at 1-800-221-7945, extension 5442,
or by email at MacmillanSpecialMarkets@macmillan.com.

First Edition: 2023

10 9 8 7 6 5 4 3 2 1